GRANDMA SERAFINA'S FAMOUS TIRAMISU

Jonathan J Samarro

BROADWAY PLAY PUBLISHING INC
New York
www.broadwayplaypublishing.com
info@broadwayplaypublishing.com

Cover art by Jennifer Sabo

I S B N: 978-0-88145-646-2

First printing: January 2016

Book design: Marie Donovan
Word processing: Microsoft Word
Typographic controls: Adobe InDesign
Typeface: Palatino
Printed and bound in the U S A

CHARACTERS & SETTING

ORLANDO D'ANGELO, *a frail octogenarian*
SERAFINA D'ANGELO, *his plump wife*
THOMAS D'ANGELO, *their conscientious grandson*

*The living room of an old, moldering garden apartment.
The wood furnishings are from a time of meticulous
craftsmanship. The sofa and cushioned armchair bear plastic
slipcovers.*

*The room is a reliquary of disintegrating porcelain figurines,
including the Infant of Prague, the Virgin Mary, and a
variety of Catholic saints—all of them chipped and worn
with an occasional broken limb or digit. Leftover palms from
Palm Sunday are tucked behind a crucifix on the wall.*

*A doorway, up center, leads to the kitchen. Another
doorway, down left, leads to a hallway. Down right is the
front door with its many dead bolts and a security chain.*

Early autumn. Several years ago.

Note: SERAFINA *and* ORLANDO *speak with thick Southern
Italian accents.*

(From the kitchen, SERAFINA *can be heard humming a Rossini aria. Her rueful voice is punctuated with the clanging of pots and pans.)*

(On the sofa, ORLANDO *is reading an Italian newspaper. His formal attire bespeaks a well-worn dignity. He wears thick, round, bi-focal, horn-rimmed glasses. His cane leans against the armrest.)*

(After a moment, he drifts into sleep, waking up abruptly with a startling snore and continuing to read as though nothing has happened.)

(He soon dozes again. His own snore rouses him. He clears his throat, rattles the paper, and refocuses on the print.)

(The third time, he fully succumbs. His head falls forward. His hands relax, and the newspaper settles onto his lap. He emits a soft snore.)

(We hear the buzz of the doorbell. ORLANDO *reacts, but does not wake up.)*

SERAFINA: *(From off stage)* O'lan'! O'lan'! Somebody at the door! ...O'lan'? *(Wiping her hands on a dishtowel, she enters from the kitchen. Her drab housedress is covered in part by an apron. She seems to walk slightly faster than her body can handle. She looks at* ORLANDO *for a moment, realizes he is sleeping.)* Hey! Wake up you! *(She claps her hands three times in quick succession.)*

ORLANDO: *(Wakes, dazed)* Heh? What happen?

SERAFINA: *(Loudly)* Somebody here! Somebody come! Somebody at the door!

(ORLANDO *shudders, stares at her with a look of confusion.*)

ORLANDO: What the hell's a matter with you? You on fire? What are you screamin' like a lunatic?!

SERAFINA: A'right. A'right. I'm a jus' tellin' you. I don' know what you gotta yell at me for.

ORLANDO: Look at you'self. You hair all over. You gotta mascarpone on you nose. And you screamin' like a lunatic.

SERAFINA: *(Wiping her nose)* I gotta cheese on my nose?

ORLANDO: Wipe you face. What the hell you cookin' now?

SERAFINA: Oh, I make so nice! The dessert! Oh, wait till you see, O'lan'! This a gonna be delish!

ORLANDO: *(Waves his hand in dismissal)* Eh, sure, sure. *(He starts to read the newspaper again.)*

SERAFINA: *(Laughing with joy)* Nice! Fresh! So good!— I'm a not gonna tell you nothin'. Issa surprise! You find out.... *(Wrings her dishtowel in excitement)* ...I haven' a made for you in so long! I can' even remember the las' time I make—

ORLANDO: I don' know why you gotta make so much food. Nobody's comin'.

SERAFINA: Hey, well. You never know. Somebody could come by.

ORLANDO: Nobody never comes.

SERAFINA: Eh, shut up you. Sta' zitt'. Somebody will come.

(The doorbell buzzes again.)

SERAFINA: See? Somebody come!

ORLANDO: *(Surprised)* Somebody here?

SERAFINA: *(Heads for the door)* I bet iss' my Salvatore!

ORLANDO: Issa definitely not Salvatore. He never come. *(Under his breath)* Un papavero alto!

(Annoyed, SERAFINA *heads back towards* ORLANDO.*)*

SERAFINA: Eh! He's a no big shot! He's a my Salvatore!

ORLANDO: Issa somebody else. Issa that damn Fuller Brush Man again. For somebody who don' do so much work, his hands are disgustin'! Filthy nails! Who would buy brushes from a man with filthy nails?! No wonder he don' do no business.

SERAFINA: He's a good boy!

ORLANDO: The Fuller Brush Man?

SERAFINA: My Salvatore. He's a good boy.

ORLANDO: Eh, sure, sure. He's a good boy. Never come to see us, he's such a good boy.

SERAFINA: I say a novena for him to come. He'll come. He's a good boy.

ORLANDO: Eh! Big shot. Lays the tiles. Too big to work in the car factory like his father. Too big for his pantaloni. Too big to come around once in a while... Not even ad ogni morte di papa.

SERAFINA: *(Waving her hand in dismissal)* Eh!

ORLANDO: Sure, sure. He got his own business, his own family, his own German car.... You believe it? A German car he buys. All my life I work for the men of the Ford Motor Company...

*(*SERAFINA *has heard this a million times. She mimics* ORLANDO *as he speaks.)*

ORLANDO: ...For almost fifty years, I screwed in every single glove compartment light bulb in every single Ford in the United States of the 'merica. And my son— No! He has to drive around in some fancy—

SERAFINA: Eh, shut up you! Sta' zitt'! Every day you say same t'ing! I gotta hear over and over and over and over—

ORLANDO: I'm a tellin' you issa not him! What would he be bothered with ol' people?!

SERAFINA: You—you leave my son alone!

(ORLANDO *and* SERAFINA *are glaring at each other. The doorbell buzzes again.*)

(*Little pause*)

ORLANDO: I was wonderin' if maybe you were gonna get the door. (*Little pause. He huffs, grabs his cane, starts to rise.*)

SERAFINA: Eh! Sdraiati!...

(SERAFINA *pushes* ORLANDO *back onto the sofa.*)

SERAFINA: ...I get it! Iss' my son come to see me. You—you can' even walk, you ol' t'ing. (*She heads toward the door.*)

ORLANDO: I'm fine now—

SERAFINA: (*Instantly heading back to the sofa*) You stay right on that couch. I'm a makin' you favorite.

ORLANDO: I'm a not hungry, Serafin'.

SERAFINA: O'lan', you have to eat. The doctor said—

ORLANDO: The doctor said, the doctor said! Eh! He don' know nothin'!

SERAFINA: Firs', I make a little antipast'. I use up all that cheese. Sure, you like. Iss' good—

ORLANDO: (*Shaking his head*) No, no—

SERAFINA: Then, nex', I have a nice a pasta e fagioli. Iss' nice. Fresh. With the beans. You like—

ORLANDO: Nothin'. No. Serafin'. Nothin'—

SERAFINA: Then, I have a nice a piece a ossu buc'. Good for the stomach, eh?

ORLANDO: I tol' you, Serafin'. I'm not hungry!

(There are three dispirited knocks on the door.)

THOMAS: *(From off)* Gran'ma?!

SERAFINA: Then I have the dessert!—

ORLANDO: Would you get the door?!

SERAFINA: Oh, boy! Wait till you see, O'lan'—

ORLANDO: Serafin', answer the door before they go away.

(SERAFINA is tenderly stroking ORLANDO's head.)

SERAFINA: Promise me you eat somet'ing, O'lan'. You don' eat not'ing, you don' get better. You need you strengths.

ORLANDO: You—you treat me like a bambino.

SERAFINA: Eh, somebody gotta take care of you. Why you don' eat? Linda, Christina, Cuma Mary, all my girlfrien's from the buildin', they cook all day long. And they husban's mangiano come cavalli.

ORLANDO: Eh! They eat like horses, now they all dead!

SERAFINA: What's a matter with you? You don' like my cookin'?

(There is a pounding on the door—though with some trepidation.)

ORLANDO: Serafin'—

SERAFINA: Promise me you eat somethin'—

THOMAS: *(From off)* Gran'ma?! Gramps?! I can hear you in there!

(Buzzes)

ORLANDO: By the time you open the door, I'll be dead.

SERAFINA: *(Admonishing)* O'lan'.

(Little pause)

ORLANDO: Okay. A'right. Fine. I eat.

(SERAFINA smiles.)

SERAFINA: Tha's my O'lan'! *(She strokes his head, kisses his scalp.)*

(Little pause)

THOMAS: *(From off)* Gran'ma!

SERAFINA: I comin'! I comin' already! Heh! *(She waddles to the front door, which is but a couple of steps away from where she was standing. Then, sweetly—)* Who is? *(Looks through the peephole)*

THOMAS: *(From off)* Gran'ma, it's me!

ORLANDO: Who is it, Serafin'?

SERAFINA: Somebody here, O'lan'. I don' know. *(She squats, looks through the mail slot.)*

SERAFINA: Who is?

THOMAS: Gran'ma?!

SERAFINA: Hey! Issa Tomaso! O'lan', issa my little Tomasino! I reco'nize a the kneecaps. *(She struggles to stand erect.)*

ORLANDO: *(Pleased)* Hey, what do you know about that!

(SERAFINA unlocks the series of dead bolts and chains.)

SERAFINA: Here we go!

ORLANDO: *(Gloating)* I was right. Iss' not Salvatore!

SERAFINA: I got it now! Aspett'!

(SERAFINA swings open the door to reveal THOMAS, a young man in tweed and slightly overgrown hair.)

THOMAS: *(Smiles, warmly)* Gran'ma!

(As THOMAS *comes through the door,* SERAFINA *hops up and down, laughing and cheering. She claps her hands and gestures for him to give her a hug.)*

SERAFINA: Hey-hey-woo-hee-hee-hee! Oh, God bless! Wee-hee!...

ORLANDO: *(Concurrently)* There he is.

*(*SERAFINA *squeezes* THOMAS, *rocking him side to side.* ORLANDO *is struggling and failing to get up off the sofa.)*

SERAFINA: ...Hee-hee! Oh, God bless!...

THOMAS: *(Asphyxiated)* Hi, Gran'ma—

SERAFINA: *(Releasing him a bit)* Issa my little Tomasino!

THOMAS: *(Gently)* I hope I'm not—

SERAFINA: *(Silences him with another embrace)* Oh, Figliolo! You here! Finally somebody come to my house! *(She shakes with laughter.)*

ORLANDO: You smotherin' the boy!

*(*SERAFINA, *hands on* THOMAS' *cheeks, withdraws just enough to admire him as she speaks.)*

SERAFINA: I haven' seen you in so long! Every day I pray Saint Anthony. "Where's a my gran'son? He lives so far away in that awful city." Oh, I so worried, Tomaso.

THOMAS: Oh, Gran'ma, I'm [fine]—

*(*SERAFINA *cuts him off with a tight hug. Meanwhile,* ORLANDO, *cane in hand, has finally made it off the sofa.)*

ORLANDO: Hey! Tomaso!

THOMAS: *(Faintly, still in captivity)* Hi, Gramps.

ORLANDO: Let go of him, Serafin'. You squeeze a the wind out of him. Give him to me.

*(*SERAFINA *releases him.* THOMAS *gasps for air. But* ORLANDO *is upon him. He grabs* THOMAS' *hand, then pulls*

*him into a manly embrace complete with claps on the back
and a soft kiss on the cheek.* SERAFINA *looks on in rapture.)*

THOMAS: *(Punctuated by the blows to his back)* How're...
you...doing...Gramps?

(ORLANDO *releases* THOMAS.)

ORLANDO: Eh, me!

(ORLANDO *slaps* THOMAS' *cheek.* THOMAS *winces, nurses
the cheek.)*

ORLANDO: I'm an old man. I keep falling down in the
bathroom on the tiles. The other day I nearly broke my
leg. Look. *(He tries to pull up his pant leg. When he realizes
his back will not accommodate him, he waves his hand in
frustration.)*

SERAFINA: *(Suddenly on the verge of tears)* Oh, Gesu
Crist'. God bless him. He always fallin'. *(She makes the
Sign of the Cross, kisses two arthritic fingers and presses
them against the lips of the statue of the Infant of Prague.)*

ORLANDO: Las' week. My ribs. *(He tries to unveil the
bruise on his ribs. Fumbling with his buttons, he groans in
frustration.)*

SERAFINA: We have to stand on the corner. Wait for
that bus jus' to get him to the doctor's. Everybody in
the whole buildin' peepin' through the curtains. See us
standin' there. Iss' terrible.

ORLANDO: Ah! The week before that! My head! Look!

(ORLANDO *shows* THOMAS *his head. The bruise is still
visible but has faded substantially.* THOMAS *audibly inhales
through his teeth.)*

THOMAS: *(To* SERAFINA*)* Why don't you put down a
rug?

ORLANDO: Believe me, I tell her a million times.
"Serafin', put down a rug." But you gran'ma? No! She
don' get no rug! And I keep fallin'.

SERAFINA: Oh, Tomaso! I so worried!

THOMAS: *(To* ORLANDO*)* Well, are you taking your cane into the bathroom?

SERAFINA: Sure, he take a that stick. But he fall anyway. I can' leave him alone for a second. He lose a the balance and the nex' t'ing you know—

THOMAS: You should take him in there, Gran'ma.

ORLANDO: *(Waving a hand in disgust at* SERAFINA*)* Eh!

SERAFINA: *(Pouting)* He don' let me.

ORLANDO: What are you gonna do? You. You young. You don' fall, but you gettin' a fat. Me. Look at me. I'm so thin. I'm like a piece a paper. But, you. Madonn'! What the hell do you eat?!

THOMAS: Uh, you know, I eat. I cook.

ORLANDO: You cook?

SERAFINA: Not like you gran'ma cooks.

THOMAS: *(To* ORLANDO*)* Yeah, I cook all the time.

ORLANDO: Obviously.

(ORLANDO *pinches the fat around* THOMAS' *middle a little too hard.)*

SERAFINA: What a you cook? Tell me.

THOMAS: *(To* SERAFINA*)* I make everything. I make—

SERAFINA: When I first move here, Tomaso, I learn to cook. I was jus' a young, fat t'ing. I didn' speak a no English. I didn' know nobody. So...I cook! Every day. All day long. I used to cook a so much, Tomaso, *lo avevo lonciare alla finestra per i cani in il vicolo. Capisce?* ...I had to throw the extras out a the window for the dogs in the alley.

(SERAFINA *laughs alone.* ORLANDO *twists his cane into the carpet.)*

(Little pause)

ORLANDO: *(To* THOMAS*)* You cook for you'self? …What, you don' have no girlfrien'?

(Little pause)

THOMAS: No, no. Not really.

(Little pause)

ORLANDO: *(Smiling)* Eh, sure, sure. You a young man. What the hell do you want with a woman? …You want lots of women! *(Little pause)* You know how I met you gran'ma?

SERAFINA: *(Claps her hands)* Sit, sit! Everybody!

*(*THOMAS *helps* ORLANDO *onto the couch.* SERAFINA *supervises.)*

SERAFINA: Watch… Watch it now…. There we go…. His legs, Tomaso. Careful.

(Once, ORLANDO *is settled,* THOMAS *and* SERAFINA *also sit.)*

ORLANDO: I tell you. I tell you how I meet…Me and you gran'ma, we went out on one date and then…I move out of the country.

SERAFINA: Issa true!

ORLANDO: I went back to Italy for a whole year. She didn' know what the hell happened to me.

SERAFINA: Issa true!

ORLANDO: *(Winking, aside to* THOMAS*)* I was a the gigolo! Heh-heh! *(He mispronounces the word "gigolo" — the first "g" as in "girl".)*

SERAFINA: *(Waving a hand in disgust)* Heh!

ORLANDO: Then I come back, and I say, "Eh! What the hell! I marry you!" You remember that, Serafin'? Fifty-three years ago.

SERAFINA: Oh, sure. I remember. I didn' know what the hell happen. I said, "Hey! What the hell happen to this guy?" Eh! Men! You wan' a some cheese, Tomaso?

ORLANDO: What's he want cheese for?! Look at him!

THOMAS: No, no. I'm fine. I just had lunch.

SERAFINA: How's a my Salvatore? How's a you father? He's a good boy, eh?

THOMAS: …Yeah. He's fine.

(Through the following, ORLANDO *squints through his glasses in confusion.)*

SERAFINA: I don' see him in so long. I don' see you. I don' see nobody. Jus' you gran'pa over there… *(She waves a disgusted hand at* ORLANDO.*)* …Eh, who the hell wan's to visit some ol' lady? *(She emits a self-pitying laugh.)*

THOMAS: Oh, Gram. Don't say that.

SERAFINA: I can' even remember the las' time I see you. I said to O'lan' the other day, "Where's that little Tomasino? I don' see him since…I don' even know."

*(*THOMAS *guiltily scratches his head.* SERAFINA *grabs his hand.)*

SERAFINA: Oh, Tomaso.

ORLANDO: You still at that school?

SERAFINA: Sure, sure. He at that school.

ORLANDO: Eh, shut up, Serafin'! I'm a talkin' to my gran'son.

THOMAS: Yeah. I'm still there, Gramps.

ORLANDO: Now, Tomaso. Tell me again. What is it you study?

THOMAS: *(Rising)* Structural engineering.

SERAFINA: Oh, sure, sure. He's a studyin' away. My Salvatore, you father, he used to study all the time. At the trade school. He'd be up all night memorizin' the tile samples from Gianelli's Har'ware Store down the street. Tha's a where he work when he was in school.

ORLANDO: *(Mumbling)* Sam Gianelli. Tirchio! Don' give nobody no breaks!—

SERAFINA: You have some cheese, Tomaso.

ORLANDO: Serafin', enough with the cheese!

THOMAS: No thanks, Gran'ma. I just ate.

SERAFINA: How come nobody 'round here never eat not'ing?!

ORLANDO: Shut up, Serafin'. He's a talkin' to me now... Now, tell me. What is it you study?

THOMAS: Structural engineering?

ORLANDO: *(Cupping his ear)* What is it?

THOMAS: *(over-enunciating)* Structural engineering.

ORLANDO: *(Nods in understanding)* Oh, yes. I see, I see. *(Little pause)* What the hell is that?!

(Little pause)

THOMAS: *(Struggling to simplify)* See— Well— Say an architect has an idea for a building. They come to me with their rough design. I look it over. The foundation, the frame, the archways, the overhangs. I see what kind of materials they're planning to use. And from that, I can let them know if it will stand. If it's build-able. Or if it will collapse into a big heap of rubble. See? ...But, it's not only that. *(With religious fervor)* I can also design things, too. Structures. That's what I really want to do—

ORLANDO: I don't know what the hell this guy's talkin' about—

THOMAS: Not houses—or—or—buildings. I mean, what's that? You walk around, you go in a room, you close the door. It's nothing. Bridges. That's what I want to design—bridges!

(Little pause)

ORLANDO: *(Squinting through his glasses)* Bridge? What? What bridge?

THOMAS: Well…I mean, none of them have been built yet.

(SERAFINA *makes sheep's eyes at* THOMAS, *not understanding a single word.)*

ORLANDO: What's he talkin'?

THOMAS: But they will…eventually…be built.

ORLANDO: *(Squinting)* What do you do?

(SERAFINA *whacks* ORLANDO's *arm, then instantly makes sheep's eyes again at* THOMAS.)

THOMAS: *(Sitting)* Also, overpasses. I can design overpasses—

ORLANDO: Why nobody jus' make a the nice car?

THOMAS: Or—Or maybe a parking garage.

ORLANDO: Eh!

THOMAS: *(Sitting up, to* SERAFINA*)* But I'd really like to design a bridge.

ORLANDO: Issa somethin' wrong with a makin' the car?

SERAFINA: Oh, I like a nice bridge, Tomaso.

ORLANDO: Shut up, Serafin'!

THOMAS: See, Gramps, to me a bridge is like… It's a sculpture. It's a…Michelangelo. It sings across a space and connects people.

ORLANDO: *(Muttering)* Is this a thin' to study?

(The following dialogue in Italian is rapid-fire.)

SERAFINA: *(Galvanized) Eh! Sta' zitt', O'lan'! Perche devi fare cosi? Non puoi lasciarlo stare?* (Hey! Shut up, Orlando! Why do you have to act like that? Can't you just leave him alone?)

ORLANDO: *Di che cosa stai parlando?* (What are you talking about?)

SERAFINA: *Hai questa idea in testa, che tutti debbano avvitare*—uh, uh, glove-compartment lightbulb! Well, *congettura che cosa? Nessuno vuole fare un lavora cosi stupido!* (You have this idea in your head that everybody should screw in glove-compartment lightbulb! Well, guess what? Nobody wants to do a stupid job like that!)

ORLANDO: *(Points to the ceiling) Paga per il soffitto al di sopra di testa!* (It paid for the ceiling over your head!)

SERAFINA: *Alcuni soffitto! Fagli fare quello che gli pare!* (Some ceiling! Let him do what he wants to do!)

(THOMAS looks on like a spectator at Wimbledon.)

ORLANDO: *Non ho detto niente. Non so nemmeno cosa sta studiando, il ragazzo.* (I didn't say anything. I don't even know what the kid does.) *(Points to THOMAS)*

SERAFINA: *Non mi stupisce che mio figlio non mi venga mai a trovare. Lo hai spinto lontano!* (It's no surprise that my son doesn't come visit us. You drive him away!)

ORLANDO: *Un papavero alto!*— (Literally: "The tall poppy!" Figuratively: "Big shot!")

SERAFINA: You and your glove-compartment lightbulb! That's why I don' ever see my son! *Avete fatto il mio Salvatore andare via e non ritornare mai!* (You made my Salvatore go away and never come back!)

ORLANDO: *(Waving his hand in dismissal)* Eh!

SERAFINA: *Se vuole sistemare le piastrelle, allora fagli sistemare le piastrelle. Ma chi si importa di quel fanno? Basto che siano felici e in buona salute! È tutto ci che conta!* (If he wants to lay the tiles, then let him lay the tiles. Who cares what they do? As long as they're happy and in good health! That's all that matters!)

ORLANDO: *Perchè non potrebbe essere funzionamento felice e sano in una fabbrica dell'automobile?* (Why couldn't he be happy and healthy working in a car factory?)

SERAFINA: *Eh! Sta' zitt'!*

ORLANDO: *Eh! Sta' zitt'*, you'self!

(ORLANDO *and* SERAFINA *suddenly become conscious of* THOMAS's *presence.*)

SERAFINA: *(Sympathetically pouting)* Oh, Figliolo. *(To* ORLANDO*)* Tomaso don' speak a no English. We speakin', and *non capisce una parola...*

ORLANDO: What are you talkin'? He speak the English.

SERAFINA: We sorry. Gran'ma sorry. *(She reaches out to caress* THOMAS' *hand.)*

(Awkward pause)

ORLANDO: You know, Tomaso, you gran'pa can' even drive no more. All the other cars honk the horns and shake a the fists... *(Demonstrates with an extended middle finger)* ...So las' year you father, he take away my license—

SERAFINA: Tomaso, you don' live a with my Salvatore no more. Now he got not'ing but big house, empty room. Nobody to fill it up. My poor Salvatore. How's a my Salvatore, Figliolo?

(Through the following, ORLANDO *squints through his glasses in confusion.)*

THOMAS: ...He's fine, Gran'ma.

SERAFINA: I don' see him in so long. I wait by the phone, I wait by the door. Not'ing. I pray a novena for him to come. Not'ing. What the hell happen to this guy? Why he don' come with you?

(*Little pause*)

THOMAS: Well...he doesn't know I'm here. I went out for a drive and decided to stop by.

SERAFINA: But why he don' come with you?

THOMAS: ...He's out working on a job.

SERAFINA: On a Sunday? My Salvatore don' work on no Sunday.

THOMAS: Well—he—I don't know. I haven't seen him all day.

SERAFINA: You jus' a said you had a the lunch.

THOMAS: He... We...I don't know.

SERAFINA: What happen, Figliolo? A somethin' iss' wrong?

THOMAS: ...No. Nothing. Nothing happened.

SERAFINA: Look at you face. You sad.

THOMAS: ...I'm not sad—

SERAFINA: (*To* ORLANDO) He's a sad.

THOMAS: I'm not sad!

SERAFINA: What a you think? You gran'ma asinine? Gran'ma knows.

THOMAS: I'm fine! Really!

SERAFINA: Sure, I see somet'ing's a wrong, and nobody tell me not'ing. Nobody eat, and nobody tell me not'ing.

THOMAS: ...Really, Gran'ma. I'm fine.

ORLANDO: Thirteen years I had that car. And still in good condition when I sold. Iss' still out there drivin' aroun'. And me, I can' even leave the God damn apartment. I'm stuck here with you gran'ma [all day long.]

SERAFINA: Eh, shut up over there! This a serious. What happen, Figliolo?! You tell me!

(Little pause)

THOMAS: *(Stands, wanders away)* Nothing, Gran'ma. We just—my father and I—we just—we had a little fight. That's all.

(THOMAS *bites his lower lip and tinkers with one of the Virgin Mary porcelain figurines. In his clumsiness, he nearly sends the figurine crashing to the floor but he rescues it at the last minute. He offers* SERAFINA *an apologetic wincing grimace.)*

SERAFINA: You have a the fight with my Salvatore?!

THOMAS: No… No… A little.

SERAFINA: *(Incredulous)* Figliolo…

THOMAS: *(To* SERAFINA*)* …I wouldn't really call it a fight…I wouldn't even call it an argument. It's more like he says whatever he wants, and I just…I sit there…I don't know what's wrong with me. *(Buries his face)*

SERAFINA: What a you talk?

THOMAS: …This morning he tells me he wants me to quit school, move back home, and take a job with him, so he can retire in a few years and leave the business to me.… And he just—he says this like it's expected of me. Like what I want for my life—that doesn't even matter. I'm not even a thought in the man's head. *(Little pause)* Well, why should I be? I just sit there. I never say anything. I never stand up to him. I never say what I want.

SERAFINA: Figliolo...

THOMAS: He doesn't understand why someone my age is still in school.

ORLANDO: *(To himself)* I don' understan' it myself. Don' make no God damn sense.

THOMAS: *(To SERAFINA)* I mean, I go to an Ivy League school. I'm the first one in our family to get this kind of education...I know, to him, it's an unfamiliar field, but I mean, I know what I'm doing.

ORLANDO: *(To himself)* I don' know what the hell he's doin'.

(Little pause)

THOMAS: *(To himself)* Why can't I talk to him? Why can't I tell him who I am—what I want?

(Little pause)

SERAFINA: Oh, don' be upset, Figliolo. He's upset. I hate the fightin'. I pray Santa Maria. Everybody be happy. No more fightin'. *(She crosses herself, kisses her fingers and presses them against the lips of the statue of the Virgin Mary.)*

ORLANDO: Serafin', go. Go away. I want to talk to the boy.

SERAFINA: I get you some cheese, Tomaso. You feel better—I got all this cheese! What the hell am I supposed to do with it? I bought it across the street at the Acme. I had to cross that awful street. Oh, Madonn'. All them cars. They don' stop for no old lady. What do they care? They run you right down. I nearly get a myself killed jus' to get a some food. You have some.

(THOMAS *nods.* SERAFINA *heads for the kitchen and without even turning to consult him*—)

SERAFINA: You wan' a the soda? I have a the soda. Have a soda.

(SERAFINA *exits into the kitchen.* ORLANDO *watches her as she goes out, then turns to* THOMAS.)

ORLANDO: Vieni quí. Vieni quí. Come here. I want to talk to you.

THOMAS: I know what you're going to say, Gramps. *(Resolute, he sits on the sofa next to his grandfather.)*

ORLANDO: She's a gone. Now I can tell you.

THOMAS: I mean, I came out here to visit. To see if for once my father and I could sit and talk and maybe have a real conversation about something. Anything. And, instead—

ORLANDO: *Eh, sta' zitt'.*

THOMAS: I mean, what does he think I am, anyway?!—

ORLANDO: Never mind what you are! Iss' about time you show up. I wait every day for somebody to show up. Finally, somebody come. Now you can rescue me.

THOMAS: …Rescue you?

ORLANDO: You come in the car?

THOMAS: …Yeah. Why?

ORLANDO: *(Grabbing his cane)* Good. Help me up! I go get a my jacket. We make a the run for it!

THOMAS: Wait—Wait a minute—

ORLANDO: I esplain a when a we get there.

THOMAS: Where are we going?

ORLANDO: I'm a comin' to live a with you!

(Little pause)

THOMAS: *(Gently grinning in confusion)* What?

ORLANDO: Sure! I got to live a with somebody and it certainly ain' that Fuller Brush Man! I'm a glad iss' you that come, Tomaso. You a good boy—

THOMAS: Live with me?—

ORLANDO: Now, go bring the car around. Quick! And then you gotta help me down a the front stoops. Otherwise I fall on the cement. Break a my head right open like an egg. Those God damn han'rails don' do no good. You got a the han'rails where you live?

THOMAS: Of course, I have—What are you talking—

ORLANDO: I jus' gotta get a one, two, couple a thin's. Nothin' too big. Don' you worry. Me. I don' take up no space. You hardly even know I there. I already pack a little suitcase I keep a hidden in the back a the hallway closet—

THOMAS: Gramps, slow down—

ORLANDO: Oh! And I gotta get a my special, secret, little a envelope I keep in the bureau drawer underneath a the socks. Somethin' my father gave me when I was a the boy. And don' you worry. Tha's all I bring.

(SERAFINA enters from the kitchen, carrying two glasses of soda.)

SERAFINA: O'lan'?!

ORLANDO: *(Startled)* What happen? *(He gives THOMAS the signal to keep this between the two of them.)*

SERAFINA: You wan' a the soda?

ORLANDO: No, no soda, Serafin'.

SERAFINA: Eh, I bring. You drink. *(She sets the glasses down on coasters, then exits into the kitchen.)*

ORLANDO: *(Huddling up with* THOMAS*) Andiamo! Andiamo! Su, andiamo!*

THOMAS: *(Concurrently)* Why are we—What— Gramps—

ORLANDO: There's no time now, Tomaso! Help me up!

(THOMAS *looks around, completely flustered. He cracks a half smile.)*

THOMAS: Gramps. You're joking. This is a joke.

ORLANDO: Issa no joke!

THOMAS: *(His smile vanishing)* Okay. Slow down. Why are we doing this?

ORLANDO: *(Groans in frustration)* Okay. A'right. Fine. I tell you. *(Looks around suspiciously)* You gran'ma… *(Little pause)* Strega.

(Little pause)

THOMAS: What?

ORLANDO: Strega! Strega!

THOMAS: I don't speak Italian, Gramps.

ORLANDO: What do you mean you don' speak Italian?! Of course you do. I taught it to you. When you were this big… *(Indicates the height of a fairy with a space between his fingers)* …Sure. You used to come and spend a the night. You so cute with you little pajamas. Gran'ma would fix up my ol' army cot like it was a you bed. Then in the morning you would wake up, wipe a the little crumbs out a you eyes and say, "Gram'pa, you teach me how to speak a like a you and Gran'ma?" You remember?

THOMAS: *(At a loss)* I, uh…

ORLANDO: *(Slipping into the past)* Oh, you such a good boy. You used to say all those beautiful words. And you used to count. Oh, how you used to count! Uno,

due, tre, uno, due, tre, uno, due—You never went pass'
tre!

THOMAS: Gramps—

ORLANDO: *(Snapping back to the present)* Heh? What
happen? Oh, yeah… You gran'ma… *(He looks around,
leans in, and whispers.)* Strega. She's a witch. She's a
tryin' to kill me.

(Little pause)

THOMAS: She's—what?

ORLANDO: Kill me! She's tryin' to kill me!

THOMAS: She's trying to kill you.

ORLANDO: Tha's a what I say!

*(SERAFINA enters from the kitchen. With each appearance,
her apron is more soiled. ORLANDO starts.)*

SERAFINA: Tomaso, you wan' a the green olives o' the
black?

THOMAS: …Uh, the black.

SERAFINA: You wan' a the ones a with the pits o' the
ones you used to put on a you little finger? *(Wiggles her
arthritic digits)*

THOMAS: Either one, Gran'ma.

SERAFINA: Eh, I bring a them both. You pick what you
like. *(She returns to the kitchen.)*

ORLANDO: *(Sadly)* You don' believe. You think I crazy
ol' man.

THOMAS: I—Gramps—I would never… Let's put your
feet up.

ORLANDO: I tell you! She's a tryin' to kill me!

THOMAS: *(Calmly)* Why do you think she's trying to kill
you?

ORLANDO: Iss' true. I know it. I seen her do.

THOMAS: What, what did you seen her do? *(He begins fluffing throw pillows and arranging them on one end of the sofa, as he continues to gently humor* ORLANDO.*)*

ORLANDO: She cooks all day long and who the hell is she cookin' for? …Nobody!

*(*THOMAS *stops fluffing.)*

THOMAS: So?

ORLANDO: So, she wraps it up. Puts it away. Waits till iss' rotten. Then she gives it to me.

THOMAS: *(Smiles, resumes fluffing)* That doesn't mean she's trying to kill you, Gramps.

ORLANDO: *(Waving a dismissive hand at him)* Eh! No girlfrien'— Of course she try to kill me. Eh, tha's what they do.

*(*THOMAS *encourages* ORLANDO *to lie down.)*

THOMAS: Come on, Gramps. You need help with your legs?—

ORLANDO: But I outsmart that ol' woman. I put a the food in my mouth. And then when she's not lookin', I spit it in a the napkin—

THOMAS: *(Hoisting* ORLANDO*'s legs onto the sofa)* Up we go!—

ORLANDO: Then I go flush it down the toilet—

THOMAS: Gramps, you just need to relax. Okay? Gramps?

*(*ORLANDO *is lying down on the sofa.* THOMAS *kneels beside him.)*

ORLANDO: *(Hurt)* You don' believe.

THOMAS: You know, maybe Gran'ma's just forgotten what it's like to cook for two people. You know, you two are alone now, and she still hasn't gotten used to it.

ORLANDO: We alone for thirty years now!

THOMAS: Okay. So, she misses my dad; she still cooks for him... *(Sits in the armchair)* ...Mom does the same thing with me. When I came home this morning, I looked in the refrigerator. You wouldn't believe how many leftovers—

ORLANDO: *(Sitting up)* Eh! Leftovers! Leftovers! Who's talkin' about leftovers? I'm a tellin' you, and you don' let me finish!

THOMAS: Okay. I'm sorry, Gramps. Go ahead.

ORLANDO: After a while of givin' me the rotten food she say, "Hey, how come this guy don' get sick and die?" So she started a puttin' the poisons. I see her. Stirrin' the rat poison right in the ricotta, the olive oil, the pesto...I miss a the pesto... *(He ponders pesto.)*

THOMAS: Gramps?

ORLANDO: You know how to make pesto? I hope you a good cook. Cause if I'm gonna be a livin' with you, believe me—

(SERAFINA hums a flourish of her aria from earlier. ORLANDO shoots a look to the kitchen door, then back to THOMAS.)

ORLANDO: You help me, Tomaso. I'm a so hungry. The only time I get to eat is when she asleep. I sneak in a the kitchen. I steal a little pinch of somethin' that looks safe. A raw egg. A sealed package of cake mix. A bouillon koob. Please, Tomaso, you have to help me.

(SERAFINA enters from the kitchen. She carries two platters overflowing with olives, roasted peppers, provolone, mozzarella—antipasti. An olive or two geronimo off the side of the plate, as she makes her way across the room.)

SERAFINA: Here we go! You come you Gran'ma Serafin' house, you eat, you feel better. No more a the fightin', Tomaso, eh?

(THOMAS *nods, smiles.*)

SERAFINA: One for you... (*Hands a platter to* ORLANDO) And one for you, Figliolo... (*Hands a platter to* THOMAS)

THOMAS: Thanks, Gran'ma.

(SERAFINA *looks at* THOMAS *for a moment.*)

SERAFINA: You such a good boy. You look a jus' a like a my Salvatore.

...He was a sittin' right in that chair when you gran'ma was a makin' twenty-three pounds a the angel hair pasta for the picnic. The pries' at the church say, "Eh! We need a twenty-three pounds a the angel hair pasta for the picnic." An' all the ladies a say, "I do it! I do it!" And the pries' a say, "No! ...We mus' ask...a Serafin'!" So I putta the flour. And I put all that dough in the machine. And I have the dryin' boards all over the house. On the beds. On the sofa there. On top the washing machine. Everywhere you look there was a the boards with the mos' beautiful angel hair laid out. And you father, he sittin' right in that chair and he say, "Mommy, you make a the house a full a angels!"... (*She is hugging herself, swaying back and forth.*) ...I look at him with his chubby little a legs and he's a got a one little a piece of raw pasta hangin' out of the mouth. I say, "Eh! What a you eatin' that raw? You gonna get sick!" "Oh, no, Mommy! I can' a wait till iss' cook! I have to eat it!" (*She laughs alone.*)

(*Little pause*)

(ORLANDO *has been squinting, adjusting his glasses, examining the contents of his platter.*)

ORLANDO: Mine looks a funny, Serafin'.

SERAFINA: Eh, shut up, O'lan'! You eat that all up! You gettin' a too thin! The doctor said—

ORLANDO: *(Waving his hand in dismissal)* Eh! What the hell he know?

(ORLANDO sets the platter partially on the coffee table. It almost crashes to the ground but SERAFINA rescues it just in time.)

SERAFINA: O'lan', you promise me!

ORLANDO: *(Waving her away)* Later, later. I'm not hungry now.

(SERAFINA claps her hands three times in quick succession.)

SERAFINA: C'mon! Eat! Eat somethin'! C'mon!

(SERAFINA picks up a piece of cheese and holds it near his mouth, cupping it with her other hand. ORLANDO waves her away.)

THOMAS: I don't think he feels well, Gran'ma.

(ORLANDO surreptitiously smiles at THOMAS.)

SERAFINA: *(Sitting)* Sure, he don' feel no good, Figliolo. He don' eat, this guy. I cook all day and what does he do? He don' eat nothin'. *(Suddenly on the verge of tears)* Then he get a the weak legs, and next t'ing you know I find him on a the bathroom floor, fallen on his head. He's a gonna drive me pazz', this guy!

ORLANDO: Shut up now, Serafin'! I don' feel good. I just want to rest a while.

SERAFINA: *(Ignoring him)* Then I take him to Doctor Delle Rosa. Such a nice man… He take me aside. He say, "Mrs D'Angelo, what's a matter with you? You don' feed you husban'?" "I feed, I feed. He don' eat. He don' like my cookin'." There's a not'ing wrong with my cookin'! When I was a young girl, I win the Sisters a Santa Maria Annual Dessert Competition four years in a row. I even got a 'cepted alla scuola culinario. I was a gonna be a the chef. 'Stead I marry this guy.—

ORLANDO: Serafin', please. Keep it down. I sick!

SERAFINA: *(Sits, teary-eyed)* Oh, Tomaso. All my girlfrien's in the buildin'—Linda, Christina, Cuma Mary—they husban's all dead. They all alone. They have nobody. Every Sunday morning, I look out the window. I watch them wait on the corner for the bus. They go to the cemetery. Tha's all they have. Now, my O'lan', he don' eat. Soon, tha's all I have.

(SERAFINA produces a dish towel from the pocket of her apron. She buries her face in the towel, sobbing.)

THOMAS: Gramps, maybe you should eat. Just a little piece of cheese. That's all. You'll feel better.

SERAFINA: *(Looking up)* O'lan', please.

(SERAFINA holds the piece of cheese up to his mouth again. ORLANDO refuses with a wave of his hands.)

ORLANDO: *(Sitting up)* Take it away. Go. Get that out of my face.

SERAFINA: *(To THOMAS)* I don' know what to do anymore! *(She buries her face in the towel again, crying.)*

THOMAS: *(Comforting her)* It's okay. He's alright.

SERAFINA: *(Angry)* You eat! Mangia! Mangia!

(SERAFINA buries her face in the towel again, crying. THOMAS gives ORLANDO an admonishing look.)

THOMAS: Gramps, just one piece of cheese, hunh? You can do that for Gran'ma. Come on…one piece.

(Little pause)

ORLANDO: Okay. A'right. Fine. I eat.

(Like a scolded child, ORLANDO takes the piece of cheese from SERAFINA'S hand, brushes it off, and puts it in his mouth; he does not swallow. She looks on in delight.)

SERAFINA: *(Bouncing up and down)* Bravo! Bravo! *Benissimo!* You make me so happy!

(SERAFINA bathes ORLANDO in kisses. He grunts and squirms away from her touch.)

ORLANDO: A'right. Don' touch. Please.

SERAFINA: *(To THOMAS)* Va bene! Va bene! Such a good boy, Tomaso. *(Sighs)* Oh, God bless! *Gesu Crist'! (She crosses herself, kisses her fingers, then presses them against the lips of the statue of the Infant of Prague.) Tutto bene!* Everyt'ing solved!

(While SERAFINA is occupied with the statue, like lightning, ORLANDO spits the cheese into a handkerchief and replaces the handkerchief in his pocket.)

ORLANDO: Somebody help me up. I got to go to the bathroom.

(Little pause)

SERAFINA: Why you got to go to the bathroom now? You only eat a one piece a the cheese.

ORLANDO: You wan' me to eat? I gotta make a the room.

(THOMAS helps ORLANDO up from the sofa.)

SERAFINA: What room you gotta make? I can' even remember the las' time I see you eat even a little a somethin'.

ORLANDO: I got to go!

(ORLANDO and THOMAS are headed off to the hallway.)

SERAFINA: *(Calling)* When you come back, you gonna eat a more cheese and you take a you pills!

ORLANDO: I don' need no pills! I'm not a sick!

SERAFINA: Tell him, Tomaso! He listen to you!

ORLANDO: You leave Tomaso alone! You do enough damage!

THOMAS: You really should take your pills, Gramps—

(ORLANDO *shakes himself free from* THOMAS's *grasp.*)

ORLANDO: Eh, shut up you! You nothin' but a screw up! Who ever heard of a grown man no job, still in school?!

(THOMAS *stands back, clearly hurt by the words.*)

SERAFINA: Don' you talk a my gran'son like that!

ORLANDO: (*Waving his hand in disgust*) Eh!

(ORLANDO *trudges down the hallway. With concern,* SERAFINA *and* THOMAS *watch him go off.*)

(*Little pause*)

THOMAS: Is he all right?

SERAFINA: Eh, don' you worry 'bout him. He don' know what he talkin' about half the time. You don' pay no 'ttention. You a good boy, eh?

(*Little pause*)

THOMAS: You know what he said to me?

SERAFINA: (*Stroking the hair from his forehead*) What? What he say, Figliolo?

THOMAS: Well… (*Laughs*) …He—

SERAFINA: Eh, sure, I know what he tol' you. He say I try to put a the poison. And now he not gonna eat nothin'.

THOMAS: …You know about this?

SERAFINA: Eh, sure. He says a the same thing to the Fuller Brush Man.

(*Little pause*)

THOMAS: He wasn't this bad the last time I came.

SERAFINA: What "bad"? What are you talkin' "bad"?

THOMAS: He looks so... *(Little pause)* How long has he been like that?

SERAFINA: Eh, he always been like that.

THOMAS: ...I mean, how long has he not been eating?

SERAFINA: Oh, that. I can' get this guy to eat. He hasn' a swallow nothin' since...I don' even know.

(Little pause)

THOMAS: Why didn't anybody tell me about this? My father—why didn't he tell me? Why doesn't he tell me anything? It's like I'm some insignificant bystander around here. *(Little pause)* Eh. Why should he tell me? I'm not even here. I'm off drawing imaginary bridges that no one's ever gonna build. I mean—who am I kidding? I should just do it. I should move back. I should move back here and work for my father. *(He stands up.)* That's what I'm gonna do. That's what I have to do. That's what I'm supposed to do. *(To SERAFINA)* Is that what I'm supposed to do?

SERAFINA: What? What are you talk?! *(She pulls him back down on the couch.)* You a good boy, Tomaso. You help. You help you gran'ma.

THOMAS: Of course. Of course I will.

SERAFINA: You gran'pa—he comes back, you say, hey! Have a one, two couple a bites, eh?

THOMAS: Of course. Two bites. It's not gonna kill him.

(Little pause)

SERAFINA: *(Reconsidering)* ...You right. Three. Three bites.

THOMAS: *(Softly)* ...Hunh?

SERAFINA: *Uno, due, tre.*—You remember how you used to count? Over and over and over. Uno, due, tre, uno, due, tre, uno, due—You only go up to tre. So cute. God bless! *(She squeezes him.)*

THOMAS: What'd you mean: three?

SERAFINA: *(Caressing his cheek)* You a good boy. You help gran'ma. Jus' cause he ol' man he's a no stupid. He's on to me.

THOMAS: Gran'ma!

SERAFINA: But you. You smart. You in that school. You can do it. He listen to you. Three bites. And that's it. *È fatta.*

THOMAS: *(To himself)* This isn't happening. It can't be.

SERAFINA: Then, we go. You take me to my Salvatore. I stay there. I move right in you ol' room.

THOMAS: So what—you're just gonna poison Gramps?

SERAFINA: Sure, sure, I put a the poison, and why not?

THOMAS: Why not?!

SERAFINA: Well, who the hell wants to live with someone like that for fifty three years? Issa not natural.

THOMAS: You can't go around killing people!

SERAFINA: Who's killing people? I kill one man. That makes me bad person? God understan's! *(She pets the head of the statue of the Infant of Prague.)* He never been married, but he understan's.

THOMAS: How could you do this?

SERAFINA: What? I jus' a stir right in a the pot.

(THOMAS collapses onto the sofa. He sits, head in hand. SERAFINA cuddles up next to him.)

SERAFINA: You know, Tomaso, when I was a the young lady, I was a gonna be a the chef. A worl' famous. Cookin' in a the fancy restaurants in a Tuscany, Rome, Hoboken. Sell my own frozen lasagna in a the

supermarket. Everybody know Serafin'. Househol'
name. So every day I in the kitchen for eleven, twelve,
eighteen hours inventin' a new recipe, perfectin' an
ol' one. I even win a the contest for my tiramisu. But
instead I end up married to you gran'pa.

(We hear a toilet bowl flush.)

SERAFINA: When O'lan' come back to marry me. I
didn' a want to get married. But my father already tol'
O'lan' I would be the wife. I didn' even a get a chance
to say nothin'. Sure I win a few contests after that. But
O'lan' say, "No! No time for contests. You gotta take
care a the baby." I say, "Eh! We don' got a no baby!"
So he give me one...And what do I end up with?
Nothing! I get a the son that never come aroun'. I get a
the gran'son, never come aroun'. I got a O'lan' who's
always around and I sick of 'im. Plus, he gettin' ol'
now. Always hurting himself. I no like to see that. Issa
not nice to see. *(Little pause)* So, I do what I have to do.

THOMAS: You can't just kill the man, Gran'ma!

SERAFINA: What am I s'pposed to do, wait it out? I
won' have no time left for me. *(Pouting, she turns from
him.)*

THOMAS: You can't blame him. You went along with it.

SERAFINA: ...And you do same a thing. Leave that
school. Come back here. Lay the tiles. Issa stupid! ...
Sure, you get married, you take over you father's
business, you listen to what everybody say. And you
end up just like you Gran'ma Serafin'.

(Little pause)

THOMAS: You're right.

SERAFINA: Of course I'm right.

THOMAS: No, no. I mean you're right.

SERAFINA: What'd I jus' a say? *(Little pause. She cuddles up to him.)* So you help a me with you Gran'pa?

THOMAS: No, Gran'ma, I'm not gonna help you poison Gramps.

SERAFINA: You no such a good boy. *(She turns her back on him.)*

(Little pause)

THOMAS: And you're gonna stop this now. *(Little pause)* It's not nice. *(Little pause)* You hear me? *(Touching her shoulder. As if to say "You hear me?")* Gran'ma?

(SERAFINA moves away from THOMAS's touch.)

(Little pause)

THOMAS: *(As if to say "Can I ask you a question?")* Gran'ma?

(SERAFINA groans.)

THOMAS: My father—How did he tell Gramps?

SERAFINA: *(Turning to him, confounded)* Tell you gran'pa? What he tell you gran'pa? What a you talk?

THOMAS: My father—I mean, he somehow managed to do what he loves. How did he tell Gramps he wasn't going to spend his life…screwing in glove compartment light bulbs? …What did he say?

SERAFINA: What he say?

THOMAS: Yeah. What did he say to Gramps? How did he tell him?

(Little pause)

SERAFINA: He don' say nothing like that.

THOMAS: What do you mean?

SERAFINA: He don' say nothing.

THOMAS: He never said anything?

SERAFINA: He don' say nothing!

(Little pause)

THOMAS: So Gramps said come work with me in the factory. And then my father—he goes out and becomes Sal the Tile King. And nothing was said?

SERAFINA: No, he don' say nothing. He jus' go. You gran'pa—he mad. You father—he mad. And nobody say nothing. What's a matter with these guys? They don' talk. They don' say nothing. They can' hardly be in a the same room. That's why my Salvatore—he hardly ever come around.

(Little pause)

THOMAS: How do these people live like that?

SERAFINA: *(Waving her hand in dismissal)* Eh.

(Little pause)

THOMAS: I'm gonna go home, and me and my father— we're gonna have a long talk. I'm not gonna spend my life like that. I'm gonna tell him, Gran'ma. I'm gonna tell him everything. Who I am and how I intend to live. And if he still wants me as a son he's gonna have to accept it.

And who knows? Once I show him how it's done, maybe he'll work things out with Gramps.... Maybe he'll come around more often.

SERAFINA: My Salvatore?

THOMAS: Uh-huh.

SERAFINA: He come around?

THOMAS: Yeah.

SERAFINA: My Salvatore coming to see me?

THOMAS: Yeah. Maybe.

SERAFINA: Now you talkin'. *Va bene! Va bene! Bravo!*

(SERAFINA *and* THOMAS *embrace.* ORLANDO *enters, carrying a suitcase and his cane. He wears a wool overcoat and a large fur hat. He walks slowly toward the sofa. She sees him.)*

SERAFINA: What's this?

ORLANDO: *(Dismissively)* Eh!

SERAFINA: He's a gotta the coat. He's a gotta the suitcase. O'lan', where the hell you goin'?

ORLANDO: I gotta sit down. Take break. Too much a the movin' aroun'.

(THOMAS *helps him onto the sofa.)*

ORLANDO: Tomaso, you go without me. I'm a not gonna make it.

SERAFINA: Where are you going?

ORLANDO: I'm a not goin' a no place, Serafin'. Where would I go? Do I ever go anywhere? The only place I go is the doctor's. And pretty soon, not even that.

(Little pause)

SERAFINA: O'lan'?

ORLANDO: What?

SERAFINA: I wan' to tell you somethin'.

ORLANDO: What?

SERAFINA: I don' put a the poison no more.

ORLANDO: What? What are you talkin'?

SERAFINA: You think I put a the poison? Well, you right. Sure. I put a the poison.

ORLANDO: I don' think nothin'.

SERAFINA: But I don' put a the poison no more, O'lan'.

ORLANDO: I don't think crazy thing. Why I think that?
I don' know what you talkin'... Put a the poison. You
crazy.

(SERAFINA *grabs* ORLANDO'*s face and kisses him.*)

ORLANDO: Hey-hey! *Va bene! Va bene!* Now that I like!

(ORLANDO *winks and with his head motions toward the*
bedroom. ORLANDO *and* SERAFINA *smile at each other.*)

SERAFINA: Now I get a the tiramisu. No poison. I jus' a
scrape it off the top. *(She exits into the kitchen.)*

ORLANDO: Tomaso, you a good boy. Come here to me.

(THOMAS *gingerly comes to him, sits beside him, and*
receives a smack on the head.)

ORLANDO: What the hell's a matter with you?! ...You
don' tell a woman thing like that! A woman issa fragile.

(From the kitchen, SERAFINA *can be heard singing an Italian*
love song.)

ORLANDO: You a gentleman. Use a you head. But,
tonight? Tonight, I get laid, eh?

(THOMAS *is embarrassed.* ORLANDO *hands* THOMAS *an*
envelope from his pocket.)

ORLANDO: Here.

(THOMAS *opens it and removes a pair of cufflinks.*)

THOMAS: What's this?

ORLANDO: You take. 'S nothing. Pair of cufflinks.
For twenty five years they stay in a the envelope
underneath a the socks. I don' use. What the hell I'm a
gonna use 'em for?

(THOMAS *examines the cufflinks in his palm. He is*
enamored of them.)

ORLANDO: My father gave a to me. Eh! Maybe you don' need no cufflinks. But who knows, maybe you put a them on a once in a while.

THOMAS: Thanks, Gramps.

ORLANDO: Don' tell you father I give.

(THOMAS *thinks for a moment, trying to remember something.*)

THOMAS: ...*Buon giorno...Mi chiamo Tomaso D'Angelo... Come stai?*

ORLANDO: Hey, what do you know about that? ... Serafina, get the hell out here! Listen to this guy!

(SERAFINA *enters from the kitchen, carrying portions of tiramisu on a tray.*)

SERAFINA: What happen? I can' leave you alone for a second.

ORLANDO: Listen to this guy.

SERAFINA: What? What a I listen?

THOMAS: *(Stands)* Buon giorno. Mi chiamo Tomaso D'Angelo. Come stai?

(THOMAS *bows.* SERAFINA *smiles.*)

SERAFINA: *Bello. Bello. Bello lui.*

(*Music swells. They begin to eat*—ORLANDO *with some initial trepidation—as the lights fade.*)

END OF PLAY

TRANSLATIONS

Ad ogni morte di papa. Every death of a pope. An idiom meaning once in a blue moon.

Andiamo. Let's go.

Antipast'. An appetizer.

Aspett'. Wait.

Bambino. A baby.

Bello. Beautiful

Bello lui. He is beautiful.

Benissimo. Great.

Bravo. Well done. Good.

Buon giorno. Good day.

Come stai? How are you?

Cuma. The name given to a godmother.

Due. Two.

Eschrole. A leafy vegetable served with beans.

Figliolo. Kid. Son.

Gesu Crist'. Jesus Christ.

Madonn'. The Virgin Mary.

Mangia. (You) eat.

Mangiano come cavalli. They eat like horses.

Mascarpone. A type of Italian cheese similar to cream cheese.

Mi chiamo... My name is...

Mortadell'. An Italian cold cut.

Ossu buc'. Veal knuckle.

Pantaloni. Pants.

Pasta e fagioli. A soup with noodles and beans.

Pazz'. Crazy.

Pesto. A sauce for pasta made from basil and garlic

*Polenta con uze*i. Corn meal with quails.

Prosciutt'. An Italian cold cut; ham.

Ricotta. A type of Italian cheese.

Sdraiati. Lay down.

Sta' zitt'. Be quiet.

Strega. Witch.

Su andiamo. We go, then.

Tiramisu. An Italian dessert.

Tre. Three.

Tutto bene. Everything is good.

Uno. one

Va bene. That's it. It's good.

www.ingramcontent.com/pod-product-compliance
Lightning Source LLC
Chambersburg PA
CBHW070035110426
42741CB00035B/2786